From Ignorance to Intelligence

Lynell Brintley

DEDICATION

For my family. Through it all we've stuck together from foster care, poverty, hurt, pain, death, sickness, and many other trials and tribulations. To my friends, thank you for not giving up on me in my dark times, though it was very difficult to make it thus far I appreciate you all for supporting me. To everyone who has inspired me to finish this book thank you, especially to Richard Patterson III, thank you for having faith in me and motivating me to pursue my dreams. To my high school teacher Ms. Cargil, I love you and thank you for speaking true words in my life consistently "Don't procrastinate", you seen the light in me and I thank you for that. To my grandmother who always makes sure I am taken care of, to my mother who cultivated the life and wisdom I use today , to my sisters who actually taught me how to read, and to my brothers who has always been there by my side in times of struggle, I love you all. This book of poetry, spoken word, and my message to the world on helping relationships blossom everything you have done in your life has lead you to this point in life, including reading this book.

INTRODUCTION

Let's be honest!!! We're all working through challenges to cope with our present circumstances. Loving your children, makes you exceptional. Doing what had to be done, opposed to what you enjoyed is not a moment but rather your lifestyle. The goal in life is to see something today that you didn't see yesterday (progress). What happens when the mind begins to say to you that your efforts don't matter and maybe those around you can't see the sacrifices you've made?

Take this Journey from Ignorance to Intelligence with Mr. Brintley as he opens up about real life perspectives. Lynell Brintley was born and raised in Detroit, MI and his roots runs deep with hard work and creativity, instilled by his mother and Grandparents who were strong in the military. Lynell discovered his gift to write as a young boy and since that time has done countless spoken word pieces, poems, creative writing and short stories.

This book will assist you in taking a different approach or perspective to your accomplishments, while empowering your future goals. See yourself as a King, embrace your beauty as a Queen and share these essential writings with a friend. Grab a copy for yourself, and maybe even a friend and let these perspectives transform your now into new possibilities that blossom into opportunities. Being optimistic is key, to combat the bad or negative things that has transpired in your life. You are more than your occupation and no matter where you are right now, things will get better because you were made to shine in darkness.

Too busy struggling
Not enough budgeting
Too much of doing nothing
Way too many assumptions
Too many people bluffing
Running late, missing discussions
A lot of poker face
Real facts yet we still debate
We speak love but we breathe hate
Living a life only to embrace fate
What's the proper way to live?
Who has the key to give?
To the youth, protect their name
Enrich their spirits protect their flame
To the old, do for them the same
Defend the helpless it doesn't change
We all need a dose of what makes each other better
as a society
Or we'll end up destroying ourselves so let's stop
the negative dichotomy

It starts with wanting to be accepted
It forms from being neglected
The desire to be respected
Yet...you're dismissed and rejected
This will either break you or make you
Habits will lead you or cause you to be reduced
Will you win when all bills are due?
Will you surrender or remain true
Your petition upon life is your result
The patterns you create is the ultimate cost
It will either create good or bad cycles
Practice patience...or repeat the same trials
Addition to being stuck in a spiral
Mentally abused from self, that's a real psycho

Characteristic ability

Message

The attention and the validation you want from other people won't ever satisfy you and it doesn't come close in comparison to the attention and validation that comes from within yourself. When you look in the mirror everyday getting ready for the day, the person in the mirror has the first and last say so about your value and validation.

You ain't "grown"
You know nothing of kundalini and tantric
You... ain't... grown
Have you even mastered the ability of own your emotions
Still manipulative
Smh
You ain't grown
Still playing games
You ain't grown
You're still a child
When you're grown communication is easy
It isn't a huge pill to swallow
You know that tight filling you get
When it's hard to speak
Yeah, maturity clears all that up

*Sit down *

Commune

We're both hurting
Yet we don't turn to each other
We turn to outside sources who do nothing but
feed our lust
See we not in love it's obvious
We're supposed to turn to each other
To heal the hurting
We're supposed to have comprehension
To heal us
We're supposed to have respect
That's exactly what we lack
Without respect how can we expect?
Anything less than the mess
We created, over and over
Yet, I'm taking full responsibility
It's my duty as a man to apply this accountability

Rushed

"Toughened up, boys don't cry"
So he wiped his eyes
Vowed to never show emotion ever again
Stop talking, go to your room
So he became an extroverted introvert
"You want to be a man don't complain"
So he looked in the mirror and said he'll never express himself.....
A single mother has to be both mom and dad
What makes it sadder is the single mother dealt with pain of her own
She didn't realize she projected the emotional toxins on to her son's
So when they grew up not expressing themselves their habit was to run away
Bottling up all emotions, even through hell and commotion
Remember, this is what they've were taught
Hold it in and be a man
Is that really a man?

Here we take an observation of how masculine women emasculate men

This isn't an attack but an intellectual approach to the divine balance between feminine and masculine

Unapologetic immaturity

Every time she said "I'm over it" but really wasn't,
her heart broke a little bit more

Ever since their first time having a major
disagreement nothing has been the same

He said you don't look at me the same, no not after
we make love, nothings the same
This is the reason he gave up
After days of reflecting of what to do
The solution was to let her go
Too many times he felt he broke her heart
That's too close to death
And he rather see her live
Happily ever after, even if it's not with him

I know sometimes we slip...but

You'd talk to your daughter with respect and honor
right?

Well that's the same way we need to speak to
women in general

...nigga you wouldn't exist without her

Yes I get it, you've been played, hurt, indirectly talked about, disrespected, etc...

But homie you got the solution

How are you going to win when you ain't right within?

Maybe you need to play the Miseducation of Lauren Hill again...

Internal

Why did you touch me?
Why did you interrupt my innocence?
My growth, my dreams, my passions
You didn't have to do that
Now I'll forever hate men
I'll forever be resentful
You took my sacred crown
Threw it to the ground
I begged you to quit
You didn't listen
You just kept destroying
I hate you

Slave Master

Message:

Do you remember ever since that day in middle school when someone cut in front of you and the inferior feeling arose in you? Do you realize you've been carrying the same bullying spirit that you were a victim of? It's unfortunate that you don't realize your victim mentally transformed into an egotistical attitude towards anyone. In some cases, situations that happen occasionally like when someone who drives really fast on the freeway and all of sudden cuts in front of you and now, you're racing against them in the spirit of competition or you feel disrespected. And even on cases, if someone takes a parking spot that you wanted at the mall, but they got it before you, a sudden emotion of anger stirs up, right? This spirit or mindset if you will, is detrimental because it's been attached to you like a leech, let it go.

You painting this picture
That you were worth the commitment
But you lied...
You robbed your spouse
And wasted their time
I see it from a mile away
You ain't ready to stay
You ain't ready to be for real
Who hurt you this bad can you tell me
Who did you this way?
That you'll harm innocent people keeping your
intentions concealed
A cycle of pain, now the streets are saying "hurt
people hurt people"
And people like you need healing
Stop painting an image like you're healed
Get the help you need and stop hurting others

*Immature *

How to love

No one sat down and taught her how to love
So how can she teach her sons?
Who will eventually grow up knowing only
dysfunction?
Functioning amongst only chaos at family functions
That ain't fun for kids neither grownups they
drunken
So abusive the children must run and hide
Yet it hurts because all they want is a better life
Instead of an abusive marriage and cheating on his
wife
And the wives ignoring the family needs
Continuing the destructive cycle in the family tree
Rotten at the roots, even the canal has no chance of
survival....
Except....through therapeutic healing which is vital
Signs of the coming life that's better
For everyone who reads a holistic letter
Written by Dr. Sebi or Queen Aufa
Many leaders to choose from that knows what to
do

Connected

Loyalty to an abusive and toxic person is emotional
suicide
Someone who doesn't reciprocate who will leave
your side
You want to be in the cycle of appreciating people
right?
Not in the society of evil doers because of spite?
Then the time is now to heal
The time is now to feel
To hold tight to who you are
Listen... and gaze among the stars
Listen... not with your ears but with your heart
See....the ending birthing a new start
Keeping you safe from the soul snatchers
Cold hearted individuals that'll serving a cold platter
Use you up
Spit you out
And never look back
So, the time is now to heal and become the warrior
who isn't afraid to attack

If only....

If only we'd realize who we are
And stop the ignorance on ourselves
If only...
If only we'd stop the mistrust and neglect
The disrespect and unnecessary drama
We're filled with trauma......
Just like they want us to be
If only...
If only we'd stop donating plasma
Taking the essential vitamins
Nutrients, minerals, and fluids
That keeps us vital and fluid
Which we are, but...
I see people walking around with bandages on their
arms like its war time...
Is it war time?
If only...
The awareness levels of our young
Were meet with the acknowledgment of the elders
If only the crime rate was lower
If only the divorce rate was obliterated
If only we'd stop...
Take the time to understand friendship...
Separate romance...
And put it in the sacred place
Where it belongs

Separate from all other access....
If only....
Only if we take the time
To take the time
To realize time is just an illusion
And with that understating
If only
We understood
Healing is available
Healing is here
If only

At this point I'm like what's the point
My brother responds:
You have to stay organized
It'll help you stay focused...
I responded:
My only focus is getting out of hell
He responded:
That's the point

See my brother
He's a keeper
Eye am my brother's keeper
He helps me up when Eye am down
And Eye protect our bond with love and light

Shut up and take this game...boy
Sitting in front of a TV like a lame...boy
Learning nothing, nothing established logically
No thinking skills developed chronologically
Just brain washed, programmed, and left out
Stuck in the crab's bucket figuring what life's about
When you were supposed to learn martial arts
The art that teaches self-control this sets you apart
From the lower man that is already inside you
And how can you be broken if you're true
The arts has the ability to teach insight and
creativity
Yet TV only presents an imagination with no ability
How can we force TV on our youth as if they aren't
important?
They aren't slaves they're valuable like gems that
have been imported
Understand the time you invest in the youth is what
happens to you in the future
So be careful how you raise the future generation
that is the next ruler

*Matrix *

If you hate yourself
You will hate your spouse
              Eventually
Committing premeditated murder
Mentally, executing your love ones
              Accidentally
All because of self-neglect
The potion to heartache
     Consequently
Is when you ignore your true feelings?
And turn away from unconditional love
The penalty
Living in desperation, looking for help
Yet, it starts with self-care, self-love
     Especially

Self - Destruction

Shame is the root cause to blame
Shame keeps us in chains
So today we are plucking up that root
With deep forgiveness of self, giving hate the boot
And acceptance of your mistakes
Love yourself and don't forget to take break
We all have a similar story
It's a shame

And in the end

You got to look or you a punk
Says society
You must have sex with her or you're gay
Says society
If you don't flirt that must means....
Says society
You don't have a nice watch you're poor
Says society
Your natural hair is unmanageable
Says society
You're stupid without a college degree
Says society
You should have at least four girlfriends
Says society
You're in need of a sugar daddy
Says society
You should sell your body for money
Says society

But what do you say?

I thought I was able to help
Knowing what I know
....I know what I knew!
Now I'm thinking it's useless....
The only thing I can do is listen to you speak
Listen to the pain you're experiencing
I hear the discomfort in your voice
I hear your concern about your life
I see in your face all is not well
I see where you need help
If I knew what I know, why are you still struggling?
Maybe what I thought I knew
I don't really know

Helpless

You're not here...
And I have this love to give to you
I have dreams and ambitions I want to achieve with
you
Yet, you're not here
Alive and doing well but we aren't together
If I knew we'd be separated like this...
I'd still love you the same
You see my love is never lame
It may be silent at times but powerful like the ocean
waves
Even after the storm has passed over
I love myself deeply so what comes out of me is
deep rooted passion
Deep rooted essence like the aroma of cinnamon
and honey

Deep rooted seeds of bliss growing flowers on my
shoulders....
But ....you're not here
The sun hasn't really been shining but the
flowers...they get water from my tears
How I wish you were here
I have so much to share...
I pray one day... we'll be able to sing together again
One day we'll laugh again so much we'll lose our
breath from the joyful memories
And then we relax from that dope time of the
dopamine's being released....
Until then I must wait in peace

Peace

Absent Love

Message:

When the class is asked how many of us have our father in our life. None of us raised our hand... you'd find the wrong in this picture but there's also right in this picture. We are all pursuing an education and seeking to better ourselves. Though the picture could be better, we aren't stuck in victimization mode.

Righteous Anger

Yes I'm angry!
 But I'm angry with righteousness
When I hear news that a woman was raped
Adding an insult to injury
Having to birth a child against her will
And on her own without a father in sight
So understand
I am furious
No woman deserves to be treated as meat
Discarded away or handled roughly
Pushed into a cycle like objects in a machine
A society that overly sexualizes
And then turn around and shames sexual
discoveries

Not the slut shaming but the sacred and secure
The females actually waiting for marriage
Those who trust their sacred alter
The women who live life
Bleeding, sometimes suffering
Providing, often sacrificing self
Praying, all the time for others
Guiding, to be left behind
....yes I am angry
How disgraceful

I wanted to die
I drove to the river
Sat in the dark
Under the stars
Looked up and asked God why
Held in the gun in my hand
Thoughts began to form
Will my family be ok?
A voice: "of course they will be, do it?"
Convincing me that it's ok to take my life
Everything will be fine
I load the gun, pulling back the chamber
I looked up to the dark sky again
.........And what I saw, my God
The stars spoke to my spirit
And what I seen before my eyes
My ancestors fighting to keep me alive

And I was able to write this poem
To prayerfully show you
To never gave in
Even when it seems there's no way to win

I won

Flip

You think the harder you drink the better you think
The more pills you pop the better your life with
Rock
The more porn you watch you're satisfied and then
you'll stop?
The more you escape from reality the less you'll
deal with now?
You're wrong but you must take responsibility
Now...
Change your lifestyle habits
Let God guide you to the promise land
The land of milk and honey
There's more to life once you stop throwing away
your life
The souls that are trapped need your help
It's your responsibility to help them
Why do you think this battle has been so long?
It has been a distraction to you and your Godly
connection
The enemy knows who you are
Do you?

Almost failed

You don't feel me
Someone else will
You don't understand me
Someone else is willing to
You don't love me
Someone else will give me the world
You don't fit my frequency
It's sad because I thought we had a thing
Children, big house, family trips, and big dreams
In reality...you were just a lesson
 Taught me not to rush but to focus on my purpose
To keep my dedication to my passion
You were good
But you weren't good enough to distract me

*Neglected love *

Why don't he see that I am hurting?
She said
I wish he could read my mind...
She thought
Why don't she see I wish she told me what?
Was going on
He said
I wish she communicated better....
He thought
... If only he pay attention to what I have going on
he'll then understand
She told her sister
....I feel like it's so many things I don't know about
her
He told his brother
....but then it happen
(They're minds finally think alike)
We need more intimacy....
...
Something they lacked
One thing left out of the connect they made
Don't forget intimacy

They exist

It's said that all women cheat
That's something I don't believe
I can see
Call me naive
Call me what you want
This belief is destructive
Causing confusion
In the hearts of men
Faithful men
Who know and trust the process
Like a rites of passage
Stop this IGNORANCE
That's exactly what it is
Ignorance because you were hurt and never healed
Misleading people knowing this far from real
There's still and will always be faithful woman
Divinely connected to the divine man

Some People don't know what loyalty looks like
I'll tell you what it doesn't look like
A person who is a passive opportunist until
someone better comes along
You know what they say "the most attractive
person is the one in the relationship right"
Be mindful of the leeches whose only objective is to
use you
Never reinforce the love but abuse you
Softly and slowly so it's undetectable
Using you as bate to get attention from other
people
Disloyalty looks like a smile in the face
Love in the eyes
And feels like good energy
But behind your back
It's the complete opposite
That's what loyalty doesn't look like

Loyalty

Right Intentions

I didn't mean to be mean
Not like that
I just needed your respect
I ended up losing that
But what I gained was insight
From the inside
Still I felt defeated
I had broken your heart
From the start we both were blind
Infatuated and eager to explore each other
We didn't have a guide though
We didn't take our time so
How the hell we supposed to know our love would
have trouble with grow
We knew it was genuine
Yet we also ignored the rules
Changed the game and switched to our own lane

Hood rats

Wired to the hood rat
They come and go
We pick and choose
They wear certain clothes
Almost no clothes
And that's why they choose
That's why we dismiss
And the concept is missed
"Oh you ain't real"
"You know you like ALL this"
......
Silence
I'll pass
you presented yourself
with no decency
No morals
No compass
that means no direction
I want to lead you
But you desire no leadership
... I'll pass

Self-Love

you've been beating yourself up
And you wonder why your heart ache
You're a sacred vessel breaking
you didn't use self-control
Choose to manipulate
Choose to Master bate
Leading people on, with no intentions to heal
Breaking the seal of pure connection from God
See it's all connected
But consistently tearing down yourself
That's destroying your soul
Lacking the patience designed to save them
The people that'll eventually save you
Healing others is healing self
But you'll never see that if you're abusing self

Screw Anxiety

Dear anxiety
Screw you
With a powerful, cordless drill
Strong enough to tighten a bridge
I'm rekindling my relationship with love
Anxiety you have done me wrong
Too many times you have used me
I'm running away from you
Running back to peace
Running back to tranquility
Running back to get my mind and sanity
Running fast as I can with my God given wings
Anxiety this is my final notice to you
We're through

LIBERATION

Everyone has an expiration date but at the end yours what will it say? Will it be an empty void of nothingness or filled with a life lived full of joy that people would be happy to illustrate. What will people say about you when you ascend to the next dimension because in 100 years it'll show if you talked more than listened

Eye am reaching down in this dark pit
Eye hear screams and eye see hands reaching for
help
My arms can't pull them up alone
Eye need help...helping them
Who will take this task with me and pull up those
downtrodden
Who will sacrifice self-pleasure and put others
before them
This dark place Eye have been before yet Eye
survived
Now it is my responsibility to reach back and save
those in need
To cultivate the strength and courage to protect the
weak
As Eye was once weak, lost, and without a vision
Undisciplined, disloyal to self, abusing the temple
eye was given

Until eye matured into the light being that Eye am,
out of darkness
Eye went from crying daily to laughing until my
heart was content, healed
Eye went from not eating anything to feasting with
joy, healed
See happiness is success, don't listen to those who
are confused
Saying having money, resources, and power is of
evil
It's how you use it, not abuse it, this is righteous to
live abundant

The Truth

Her story

....She wrote her way into History
......*She spoke wisdom in the ears of the great Kings*
.......*She lives in the minds of those who seek knowledge*
.......*she has inner standing of self*
....*She is everlasting*
The first shall be last and the last shall be first

She is eternal, forever....

She is....
She exists...
She is the butterfly....
That is now flourishing......
......She didn't give up
The last shall be first and the first shall be last

Inner Love

You're allowing yourself to get infected
Due to the lack of affection
You feel lost and no direction
Well, with an immature life that's expected
With an immature spouse you never rejected
You choose to stay, you choose to be reckless
A mindset to do better, cultivates from the thoughts
To see your life better cultivating the goodness it
brought
The goodness it brings, like spring time flowers
from the seeds bought
Healthy investments now you see what she sought
Now you see why he stayed and fought
Fighting for commitment it's easy to get caught
Slipping up the stairs as funny as it is
But it's serious how we treat each other do you
want harmony or toxins
Living stressed out, locked in and boxed in
TV controlling your subconscious so you stuck on a
low level relationship

With everything you're encountering
Where is your consciousness?
Not the popularity contest of witty intelligence
But the true aura of a God the true inner being of
Goddesses
Look what time it is
Not on your wrist or phone but your biological tic
tock let's rewind a bit
Ease off the junk food and Netflix
Sex addition and sex attention
Demons craving your life source distracting you
from your business
Causing low self-esteem but that's for self to be a
critic
So again, let no man or woman infect you but you
show yourself the right things
Put yourself first not out of selfishness but
choosing to live righteously

*Right way *

Love is not manipulating
Being submissive is supporting
I care for you
I understand your vision
I therefore submit to you
When a wife submits
When a husband submits
They push each other
They become one
They become peace
They become profound
As the Moon compliments the stars
So does two lovers intertwining in this here space of
life

In your imagination
you projected yourself into the future
and you see yourself as successful
now at this present moment, you are successful
Now you over stand the importance of envisioning
yourself
In a greater light
This is a concept of creating the world that you
desire to live in
Trusting the process of knowing your purpose
The most important day is the when you find out
who you are
And why you are here on this earth

The day

The bus driver

She's seen it all
Grown man crying tears
Children in the bodies of adults
They never got a chance to grow up

The bus driver
She's seen children abused
Talked down to
Hungry
Thirsty
Made fun of because of their clothes

The bus driver
She's seen old women lost and confused
Old men hurt and cold
Young men jaded and ready to die
Young women abandoned with no guidance

The bus driver
She's seen it all
The doctor on her way to work
The students on their way to school
The prospect traveling to the interview
The mother with 3 children going home
With groceries, while pushing a stroller

She's seen it all
She looks back into her rear view
Most passengers stare out of the windows
Looking for hope looking for an answer

We sit in this energy recovering from life
enjoying the silent and beautiful sites
Mesmerizing at the cosmos of space observing the
science behind the waves
Listening for God seeing the patterns in our brain
Life is continuous because of its energies
never depleting continuing through centuries
And generations to generations generating witty
ideas connecting the planet
The magnificent joy of being one with nature taking
nothing for granted
Is total bliss and peace that pass all understanding
no reason to ask why?
Honestly what's to question when you're at peace
with The Most High

Everlasting

Liberation

They wanted you to feel ashamed of your skin
They wanted to subliminally attack your
subconscious
That deep scare they wanted to cut
That emotional wound they attempted to form
Like Leeches they wanted to drain you because of
your beauty
Your wisdom they wanted to rob you of
Your clarity they wanted to leave you lost
Without a map, without food or water, without
God without yourself
Lost within left for no one to find you equation to
division and destruction
However, you're of the light, born from the Sun
and raised by the moon
Indigo child, deep melody is in your soul
So even in the mist of confusion you find yourself
Singing hymns, the deep rooted soul songs
The songs that got you through the chaos
Even when your energy was at its lowest
Your courage and integrity did not fail you
They wanted you to choose their lifestyle but you
choose your own

*No room to cry *

Turned both ways, reality I can't face but one day I
must
At the Moon I smile, at the Sun I laugh but still no
crutch
At dawn my soul hangs in the balance, the trees
move with the wind
The sea thrusts against the land & the Earth
continues to spin
The magnitude of nature whispers in my ear
Listen my child you have a bright future here
Do not fear the emptiness when dust finally appears
For in this moment of stillness Eye have changed
the atmosphere
Do not neglect the frontier, adhere to the stars that
are present
Eye have given this to ALL, to gaze upon the
firmament

My Eye Phone on 5%....
Walking this road home, and its cold
I'm taking this as sign from the Most High
Telling me to put my phone down and get in tune...
With Cellf, you inner stand?
I am you and you are eye...
Says the Most High
Especially when my eyes have been focused on the
light
That shines across the whole universe
like a verse written in the skies
straight from the Most High, damn an alumni
if I can't even get my life right
it starts with building upon my health
Stealth, Demons can't see me the mode eye am in
No more darkness except the divine darkness
Would you curse the stars because they're
surrounded by darkness

Exactly

Control

They told you that you must be HYPER
MASCULINE but they lied to you in the same line
Being hyper masculine destroys the balance of the
feminine at the same time
The need to strike fear in others to feel powerful
Yet you don't adapt to healing you only know
survival
No.. We weren't taught to pursue sex in Order to
find an identity
Yes... it's meant to be creative and made to create
divinely   only the responsible and mature
adults can do this sex thing
But in the back of your mind the only thing you
look for is the whore in a Queen
Stop trying to blame society for what you didn't
learn but you know right from wrong
Even 2Pac said it's time we heal our women be real
to our woman what a pivotal song
Besides that you was only told that giving women
sex and money is the only thing that is satisfying

Yet that's far from the truth because that only
satisfies women who souls are dying
Dumb, no purpose in life because no one took the
time and now here you come along "not shining
light"
Only offering sex as an answer shaking my head
you're so far from bright
As a man your job is to protect and project the
energy of confidence
Rather that's helping the old or teaching the youth
common sense We all face adversity praying to
make it the next day   Hustling to pay
bills righteously living a different way
Than what Willie Lynch drew up for the negro race
Now see and understand we don't have to choose a
destructive gate
Study the martial arts see what it did for Bruce Lee
Walk the other way and practice self-mastery

1st Law

Self-preservation is the key to life
it holds the power to set you free when you sleep at
night   if you abuse life then life abuses
you   cycle of
love and the Universe is helping you make it
through   yet if you wish to live in bondage
and become a prisoner of life   go ahead abuse
yourself forget the gifts and live in strife
forget the jewels that have been planted in your
mind from birth   Forget the thrown that
was built to bestow your worth   Life is
full of twist and twirls so you have to prepare your
soul   for the battle is already won but you must
be indubitably whole   like your inner fire in the
tomb of your body waiting to be resurrected
don't abuse what God has given, all your ways are
directed   Through life trials and tribulations
they won't attach a strong hold One thing you must
know, victory in battles are lessons to be told

while avoiding the snakes, thorns and things thrown
to distract and destroy
Essentially it is a part of the process cultivating
maturity because you aren't a toy
Made to be played and tossed around, I don't think
so Only if they knew the weight of the crown, I
think it's time we let them know

Complement

Love is not manipulating
Something weak minded individuals don't
understand
being submissive is supporting
you care for me? Showing me is a better plan
I understand your vision
I can submit to you yes even on demand
when a wife submits
a husband concurs and expands the land
they push each other
they become one band
they become peace
Drumming with a sound heart hand and hand
Fighting against each other no longer
A woman truly cultivates a man
A natural flow
Like a cleansing waterfall and under it we stand
Don't compete
Compliment and cherish

My Wish

Eye pray your worse days pass away......

Ya better days increase and your success starts
today.....
May your eyes no longer be worried and your stress
decay.....
And may your heart be filled with joy and your
mind in tune with God ways
May your joy increase daily and your heart
strengthens
Let your love grow abundantly forever in richness
Let your hair be flawless and your body void of
sickness
Eye pray your prayers are answered with a powerful
quickness
And may your light shine on, on and on

Forever into eternity reflecting a beauty dawn

When I realized taking a selfie with the flash
pointing towards me was the same as looking up to
the stars and smiling

I figured I was halfway to the mark of innerstaning,
the true essence of life and that was discovering self
through nature

We all came through Mother Nature, that day your body was taken out the womb of your mother and placed in her hands

Is equivalent to God taking a star directly from the outer space and placing it in your hands....

The contacts in my eyes like contacts in my phone gained value when Eye realized enlightenment after eye opened my eyes

Like an extraterrestrial calling me on my cell and telling me "I'm with you" don't be afraid

For wherever you go I will be present with you on this plain

Mixed emotions I drove straight without distractions because the message had me smiling like on Christmas Day

No not the fake reason we celebrate but the kind acts that have humans acting kindly

Not blindly or out of control but through understanding we are made to love

Like two doves multiplied by two that's the power of me and you

The world is a beautiful place made for beautiful people

Like painting a picture for the next generations to learn from what we are experiencing currently

Like a museum filled with articles, artifacts, ancient routes, and underground communication

Just like Harriet's chariots and the Marcus Garvey army

Study to show thy Cell approved, like a body energized ready to move

Reflection

Risky

You risk your life just to get attention

Selling your soul for the wrong type of affection

Unhealthy attention can bring you universal hell

That's like breaking into prison, pointless

Feeling lost and hopeless

You equated fun with connected to the wrong

You disregard wisdom and reject the strong

At the end of the day

You wonder why you feel sick and depleted

You gave your life over to ill ways

The only way out

Is the way in came in

Innocent, pure, and full of life

A true King is strong but gentle

Brave enough to heal your pain and increase the knowledge in your mental

To give you instructions with proper guidance filled with wisdom

A true King knows when to submit and be humble with the weight of his kingdom

A true King acknowledges his mishaps and makes petitions to take ownership of his mistakes

A true King knows how to cover you with a warm embrace

A man that doesn't belittle you but uplifts your soul and respects your space

He protects your life because knows anything less is a disgrace

He never makes you fill a void that's his

responsibility

A King who treasures your presence and protects your stability

He knows a value of a pure relationship always using humility

He understands some days are bad so he refrains from us hostility

A true King who there's a time and a place for showing strength

Calm and patient like a Lion but he ain't no wimp

If needed he'll transform into the warrior that's heaven sent

A true King who isn't afraid of love because built to be resilient

True King

You awaken my taste buds
I had no idea
You introduced me to another of euphoria
I can be myself with you
Open and transparent
Vulnerable and free
Yet, powerful enough to be interdependent
You're so radiant and magnificent
The love you give to me it's like a rare gem
My trust in you never faints never fails
You get me high on love and no reason to come
down
No relapse because we're pure hearted beings
Angelical and magical we explode supernaturally
with magic
Your simple touches are graceful sending tingling to
my spine
Awakening my inner G increasing my energy
And your message is clear
You desire to be one with me
And I am forever grateful accepting wholesomely

New life

I'm not about to belittle you or me
What I value is high self-esteem
Sex is a sexual energy exchange
So what I value and what you value must be the
same
Listen...you don't have to run up your body count
to be accepted
All because the pressure and the feeling of being
neglected
Pay attention to what society wants to project
See how the fathers are being removed yet their job
is to protect
So the mothers feel empty and alone like being on
an island
Guess that how Christopher Columbus said he
"found it"
Easily to be taken, manipulated , lied to and abused
See, you're not lost treasure you're not oblivious or
confused
You are physically inclined and spiritually in tune
So allowing just anybody into your space into your
womb

Is a key to destruction a key to being ruled
Now you're life is ruined but you must pay dues
Controlled by the powers that be, due to lack of
self-control
Align with the most High so that you will be whole
Instead of losing your most precious energy and
misplacing your soul
Respect yourself and the God that you hold

Images

Heavy Love

She isn't my opposite she is my compliment
Eye am her Sun she is my moon, its sent from
Heaven
When she is in my presence Eye adore her
When she is out of my presence my mind body and
soul calls for her
Her inner G compliments my inner G
She is what I imagine in my imagination because
Eye Am building a nation with her
Eye am the stem and she is the flower
I look up at her with Sunlight giving her insight
I cultivate her soul with action and passion
Lacking nothing because our minds are
continuously attracting
I embrace her like the universe embraces the earth
I don't try to understand her, she gracefully reveals
herself to me
She loves herself and I love myself we blossom
Accepting each other consciously and
subconsciously

I read her mind and she read mine
We liberate together, elevate together, climax at the
highest form, and still find ways to do it better
When I look into her eyes the universe is reflecting
Authentic connection, her third eye meets my
unspoken direction
Her body language is multilingual and yet eye know
them all
Eye contact her and she is mentally stimulated
energy flows like a waterfall
I listen to her vibes and eye feel her energy
I fill her up from her crown to the parts within her
that are deep...

My world

I don't want your sex, I want your insight
I don't need your attitude, I need your patience
I need your friendship, be my confidant
You are not my enemy, you are not my concubine
I need your beautiful voice, which heals my soul
I need your caressing words to make me whole
See, I walked these streets and it broke my heart

To see many people in need, in search of
themselves and in a higher power
That guided them to everlasting love and happiness
...See Empress, see Queen, see Princess, see Sister
I see that in you
So I humbly bow down to your presence
With respect because I know that you've been
rejected

Disrespected, Disregarded, malnourished, ignored,
called a bitch, a whore, a waste time, toxic, slut....
YET YOU STAYED SOLID THROUGH IT ALL
My God....how you endured so much yet still hold
the capacity to love

Birthing a baby, birthing a nation, birthing multiple
generations but before that going through pain
indescribable
I thank you
So when I say I need you, I'm saying the same thing
Jill Scott sang about "I need you"
Without you my sister, I am nothing
Without you mother, I am nothing
Without you my Empress, I am nothing

Lack of misogyny

Misogyny isn't the complete version of human
beings

It's actually the opposite of the true form of
harmony

It is the lack of guidance and the result of low
vibrational energy

The loss of self and the reflection of a false identity

It's the lack of love and absence of respect

It's a culture full of hate and a society living
unchecked

Leaving a residue of negativity on the platforms
that's wrecked

Can't you see that the disregard of the woman will
leave you wrecked?

The divine feminine energy created to be a creator

Yet you lack the intelligence to cultivate her

Where did society go wrong, when it became
dismissive of the translator?

Who is the divine woman designed to be the
incubator

Happy Time

I sat down with time
We made an agreement to stop fighting
I said I'd stop complaining so much

And time said it'll always respect me
Only if I respect myself
Then I asked time one more thing
I asked time. How do I find true happiness?
Time laughed and replied....
Be still and be happy and in that moment imagine
time doesn't exist

Salute

Salute to the women taking college exams and still
having babies
Salute to the women raising kids on they own
dealing with situations that's crazy
To the women who are living single pursuing a
college education
To the entrepreneur woman striving to obtain life
better than basic
The women who's working within the system
seeking to change it
Respect to the women who's working a 9 to 5
praying to make it
In this world that's so misogynistic
Where some men hate the female gender and use
them for a quick fix
Tricks is what they call them but you're the mass
manipulator

Preying on the unprotected like an infected
predator
Knowing that the female gender has disadvantages
But this type of thinking is a cause to major
damages
To the world,
To the woman striving and doing their best
You're going to make it no matter the test
I salute you and I know you can make it through
Pretty wings that you have you'll make it in jeans or
a business suit

Not It

If it hurts too much it's not love
Love allows healing and no one's above
The law which is Love there's only 1
Rule to cherish not to crush no not one
Some still lacking healing so they're stuck
In a identity of hurt and pain yet they don't say
when it's enough
Pushing away people ....when connecting is needed
Like a doctor doing surgery on an artery that's
bleeding
Desperately seeking to save a life of an innocent
body
Spiritually and emotionally they have been
wounded, oddly
Still surviving but haven't taken the time to heal
Wounded
Needing love and affection from people but isn't
loving self-Wounded
Striving to be a better version but the past hurts
...really hurts so progression keeps them....breathing
deep, but not healing your wounds

......its compassion... and love. And empathy that
clears the path and shines light on the hurt
So the healer can see where improvements need to
be...
and now it works
You start to believe
Now you are free
Now you see
Your eyes are no longer blinded
That throne is gone ..it isn't hiding
It's no longer causing neck pain or back pain
Your smile has come back and you rest well
throughout the rain
All because love covers a multitude of sins and
now....you're back right
Sin is just a long distance relationship with The
Most High
But oh how faithful love is giving sight to the blind
How a close relationship between self and love
provides
All that is needed to heal and survive
I said all that is needed to ...heal... and.. Survive

Breath

The exhale is not more important than the inhale....
However...
The inhale doesn't out rank the exhale
It's an equal exchange
Like lying next to each other
You breathing in, I'm breathing out
I'm breathing in, you breathing out
We reflect the plants in the sunlight
Absorbing energy and giving out pure energy
A sacred energy exchange that's not seen with the
human eye
Yet it's felt, deeply
So deeply the whole body reacts
The lungs smile, the kidneys dance, the livers
laughs, the stomach embraces the love, the brain is
audience enjoying the whole show and our sacred
areas await the reward of it all

Yoked

Be with someone who adores you
Someone who understands that you change
The adaptation phase is beautiful and it's a part of
the process of life
Be with someone who laughs at your corny jokes
And laughs hysterically after a huge argument
Making the wounds heal
Laughter does good like a medicine
And hugs of love erases the pain
Rain comes and go but love stays
Committed to each other and manifesting greater
Be with someone who enjoys your silence just as
much as your talking
Both are forms of heathy communication creating
true balance

Be with someone who inner stands, understands,
and over stands who you are
And never purposely miscommunicates and
manipulates their ideas
Become one with the person who prays for you
Cares for you externally and internally
Be with the one who is a soul mate to your soul
And who helps build the vision of God

<u>HER</u>

You have to know her
Feel her and fill her
Know what makes her tic, like a clock and keep it in rotation
Like the flowers, the sweet kisses, and full body massages but that's just the basics
From day one show her you're the one
If you aren't move out her way don't be a punk
This ain't a responsibility for the weak
You don't want to step to her if you can't take the heat
She's willing to submit but you got to be able to do more than just speak
Walk it like you talk it but actions speak louder than words now you see
The vision that she has for her life is beyond your wildest dream
This is why the woman is the ultimate balance but be careful she's like hot tea

Take it slow but not slow you have to vibe with her
frequency
Frequently while also balancing yourself and that's
the law of reciprocity
You have to know her, feel her and fill her
Each need meet not letting the void occur

In to You

I'll bring your fantasy into reality
this isn't lust or vain chemistry
our spirits connect like neurotransmitters in
psychology
floating in the waves of eternity of everlasting
anatomy
the stars align when we connect there is no stress
God made this a part of His plan and on the
seventh He rest
the atmosphere can't contain what we have. Not the
North, not the south, the east, or the west
Gifted, yes, even angels came to witness
The passion created by two souls it's a perfect fit
Our souls dance with one another, light footed as
we can be
Our bodies weightless as we caress each other
continuously ascending
No limits no barriers there is a hidden treasure in us
and it's never ending

Carefully

I treat her like the new book I just got
Not wanting to rip the pages
Slightly turning them
Ever so gently
Smelling the aroma
Enjoying the newness
The presence of her present
I feel refreshed in her I find myself
Diving deeply involved and evolving into one
She got me
Sprung but I got her as well
Drinking from her well
Well I was thirsty at the time and she quenched my
thirst
No longer do I seek another woman
She fulfilled what I was longing for
For a long time I searched, even google couldn't
help

Majestically she appeared out of nowhere
thin air, it had to be because she took my breath for
a second
but in that next minute she gave me life
reassured me that everything is going to be alright

My Goddess

I worship you
even in idle time
No idols come before you
I don't care what American Idol said but
you my prize possession
Possessive? A little bit but more like territorial
This pedestal I built for you fits only you
And for me you did the same things
That's why we coexist not just exist
If that was the case we both would've been at the
exit
Saying screw this because we both value our time
But even more we value our life
And it's way too short to be in a long term
relationship that ain't moving
No where can we compare because we don't
compete
In our own lane so it limited distractions
And that's rare to honest
We're kind of close to perfect but that's my opinion
No one is perfect but your perfect for me

Dream Work

Let's make it happen, let's put the groundwork in
It's good to imagine but don't get stuck being
imaginative
Hoping for money to be in your bank like the
struggle is going to magically end
You need to make a game plan and actually get in
Wealth is a mindset that must be generational
Just like we teach the bible, we need to teach
occupational
Like real estate not fake assets thinking it'll make a
profit
Teaching our children at a young age to increase in
their logic
Like mathematics, science, minerals, and gold
The industrial language we must possess and hold
Creating a market & becoming an asset

Not just living life and getting the government kick
back
Getting involved in group economics is essential
Just like following a new trend follow your dreams
with a pencil
Like writing down your vision, and following your
heart
It's up to us to give our children a future start
Like monopoly we see the major components in life
So learn to gain commodity and get your life right

Attraction

The Bee doesn't get jealous of the bird

And the bird doesn't get envious of the honey

All fear is the foundation of al imbalance

Like hate, spite, malice, contention and rebellion

There is no reason to concern yourself

Rather you exist or if you persist

Life is created to live in total bliss

Harmony filled interactions

As a hummingbird extracts nectar from the
brightness flowers

More flowers grow, attracting the love essence

Sweet honey from the bee, songs ringing from the
robin

The river doesn't reject the ocean

It flows concurrent without resistance

This is the example from the earth

This is the example foe human nature

Follow this example

Nature's law

A message to all woman

You are beautiful

Strong

Creative

Intelligent

Your vibes are vibrant

Your energy is magnificent

Your glow is spontaneous

Your joy contagious

You are loved

Cherished and celebrated

You're smart

You're brave

You are protected (Thank you)

Reason

Eye love because I know how it feels to be abandoned

Eye protect because I know how it is to be hurt

Eye pray because I know how it is to be someone's angel

Eye seek because I was once lost

Eye cry because holding back only adds more stress and frustration

Eye meditate because I know how it is to feel confused

Eye create peaceful environments because I've experienced chaos

Eye write because one day someone will read this and find life in these words

Eye sing because as free as Eye am, someone else will be free

How dare you

How dare you walk outside and not be grateful...
some of your ancestors were forced to stay inside
that's real chastity

How dare you
Neglect the wisdom given about the system, with all
the insight given to you and all the knowledge you
obtained

How dare you
Laugh at that melanin person's pain, especially
when your history is the same

How dare you
Mislead women into thinking that you truly love
them

How dare you
Look at the stars and not see inspiration, or look at
the Sun and not see dedication

How dare you
Make a statement disrespecting your ancestors, like
they didn't make sacrifices to restore your
foundation

How dare you
Walk in the shoes of the righteous and do evil
things, as if they didn't help you grow these wings,
which every black person fly on, the reason we can
safely get home

Cops

Dear Mr. and Ms. police officer why do you fear us so much

Is it because of what the media says that influence you to be blunt

To be harsh with your words and physically abuse us

Why do you treat us like we are nothing and look at us with no trust

What makes you want to release your rage upon a generation of babies who don't deserve that pain?

Why do you find fault in an innocent culture who has been taught to stay out that lane?

Yet you provoke us with weaponized mind games

It's not a secret you secretly want to be us, instead you call us lame

It's not a secret that your career deals with a lot of pressure

Some of us admire you and we desire to do better

So I decided to sit down and write this short letter

I am letting you know we are tired of the stormy weather

I am writing you today on behave of my generation

*Please stop with the violence, the lack of patience, and
the hating*

We are gifted, talented and wise children that are not fading

*We didn't create this world, only born into an
earth that needed saving*

Alien Love

Holding grudges and spiritual debt

Forming Blockages of stress

Causing you to miss a step

In your destiny which equals regret

Your reception from the universe will be hindered

No direct communication yet you want direct
stimulation to rendered
Not until you let go and become wholesomely
centered
With yourself first that's full of love strong and
tinder
One must realize that holding negativity serves no
purpose
Without direction that negativity will turn your soul
worthless
Causing a catastrophic event in your life leaving you
with curses
So release the hate and embrace the love as the
stress disperses

Conversation With them

I said I was going to stop

This time I'm serious
I put that on my love ones
I'll do it for them
Yes, that way I'll feel some type of responsibility

......Yes
Just one more time...

No

Come on its only one more time

Listen closely are you sure?

Yeah it'll be fun... AND... You don't have to go all
the way.....

Okay.....

...this is the path to deceiving yourself
Thinking you're okay with just another time saying
to yourself "I'll be alright ". Setting priorities is the
only way to be free.
I guarantee
It'll be the last time....

What is SIN

Sin is suffering in nature
Saints Indulging in Narcissism
Sunlight Immersing Never
Sisters Ignorantly Needless
Saving Illiterate Normally
Saying Instrumental Negatively
Severing Interconnections Nocturnally
Several Insecurities Nationwide
Sappy Insightful Neighbors
Sorry Integrity Notations
Seriously Ignoring Nirvana

So we see SIN is something we don't want

Keep in my mind I'm an artist

So let me test this thing out...

It's said what you do frequently becomes your
frequency
Then I must think wealth, eat wealth, think of
wealth even in my sleep
And in my dreams I'll be in my highest peek
Consistently 24/7, 365 all the days that I breath

So if wealthy is what I want to be
Then it is wealth that I must seek
See, this conceptuality can be a hard task at times
It's easier said than done more complicated than
writing rhymes
Though poetry is connected to wealth and living in
my prime
It's the metaphysical and physical plan I must
design
For my children's children who won't be fighting
over a nickel and a dime
What I do now sets an everlasting imprint in time
So wealth is the key and it all starts and ends in the
Mind

Online intellectual

We're all online
On the timeline
Exit out the app and open it 10 seconds later
No wonder it's a profit to project an image of
greater

No wonder it's called new age slavery
On line with false hopes and a false reality
Access to social media and all of society
But when you put your phone down you're hit with
the real scene
Here's your reality, you're a new age drug user
getting high on dopamine
You're a new age human distracted and stuck in
poverty
you're a new age slave stuck in the envy wave
No books so you can't even turn the page
Got your head down in church but not to pray
Pastor preaching his heart out but still can't keep
them safe
A disadvantage of people taking advantage because
men aren't in place

Each weak individual can be plucked that's a field
day for Satan
Sending innocent bodies to prison when they need
education
Real eyes recognize these times a fake lives
So realize what you giving your attention to before
you die
Blue screen on your phone and on your tv
Radiation on your phone disguised as 4G
If you're glued to your phone you need to wake up
Even your body is screaming like Mother Earth is
stuck
Even the bees are dying by the trillions such a sad
case
Who's ready to evolve amongst the people not just
a race
Distractions are more prevalent now more than
ever
Who's going to take a stand for self-love and do
better

Standing

In the face of adversity
I am knowledgeable
I am fearless
I am bright and witty

In the face a disaster
I am brave
I am enlightened
I am strong even if no one is with me

In the face of pain
I am strong
I am vigorous
I am victorious

In the face of heartache
I am persistent
I am a warrior
I am a healer

Coiled hair

Your hair continuously strengthens in a universal
circle
And I love it
Some call it nappy but I call it natural
The way your hair spirals like a whirlpool
It excites me, every time I'm around you I get
enlightened
I guess that's why they love our hair
Pressed out with a hot comb or after a shampoo;
oiled and left to be free
Rather it's short, long, nappy, or curly
I love your hair

Gaze

Isn't it beautiful
How the Sun rises early with a calm brightness
Isn't is beautiful
How the Sun sets with the same
Isn't it beautiful how the Moon shares this space
And the stars witness it all
Isn't is beautiful how the other planets cooperate
together
Teaching us from a far that it doesn't matter how
different you are
What matters
Is recognizing the beauty in each other.

Lynell Brintley
Can be contacted for book signings, Poetry
Nights and Life Empowerment Sessions by
visiting one of the websites below for more
details.

INFITEPOETRY LLC
Indigoaquarius23@gmail.com
Infinite1Poet.Com

Made in the USA
Columbia, SC
31 January 2021